AFFECT AND EMOTION

A BRIEF PSYCHOANALYTIC TOUR

GRAHAM MUSIC

Mind-Nurturing Books

Published in 2022 by Mind-Nurturing Books
90 Huddleston Road, London, N7 0EG

Copyright © 2022 Graham Music.

A first edition of this book was published by Icon Books in 2001, who have reverted the copyright to Mind-Nurturing books.

The right of Graham Music to be identified as the author of this work has been asserted in accordance with sections 77 and 78 of the Copyright, Designs and Patents Act 1988.

All rights reserved. No part of this book may be reprinted or reproduced or utilised in any form or by any electronic, mechanical, or other means, now known or hereafter invented, including photocopying and recording, or in any information storage or retrieval system, without permission in writing from the publishers.

British Library Cataloguing-in-Publication Data
A catalogue record for this book is available from the British Library.
ISBN: (pbk) 978-1-7398147-4-8
ISBN: (ebk) 978-1-7398147-5-5

Contents

Forward to the new edition i

About the author iii

1. INTRODUCTION 1

2. EARLY EXPERIENCE AND EMOTIONAL STATES 9

3. URGES AND INSTINCTS 19

4. MANAGING LOSS 27

5. NEGLECT 33

6. TRAUMA 41

7. CUT OFF FROM FEELINGS 49

8. FLOODED BY FEELINGS 57

9. THROWING STONES FROM GLASS HOUSES 63

10. THE EMOTIONAL BODY 69

11. GET HAPPY 75

12. CONCLUSIONS 81

Dedication 86

Acknowledgements 87

References 88

FORWARD TO THE NEW EDITION

This short book was originally part of a series commissioned by the Freud Museum, edited by Ivan Ward and published by Icon books. These books are, in effect, short guides.

The aim of the series was to present key psychoanalytic concepts in easily digestible formats so that interested readers, whether general readers, parents, therapists or other professionals, can familiarize themselves with a subject.

I was in illustrious company when the original volumes came out, and I would urge readers to check out others in the series by the likes of writers such as Christopher Bollas (on Free Association), Ricky Emanuel (on Anxiety), Robert Young (on the Oedipus Complex), Priscilla Roth (on The Superego), Jeremy Holmes (on Narcissism and also on Depression), Phil Mollon (on the Unconscious), Brett Kahr (on

Exhibitionism), Ivan Ward (on Castration) and several more.

When the copyright reverted and on re-reading this book, I decided to reprint it as I thought it had stood the test of time. Thus, it keeps much of its original form, but with some errors corrected, references updated and some rewriting and extra chapters.

Each section takes a theme and briefly unpacks it, for example, looking at what we mean by being overwhelmed by feelings, or by being too distant from them or by projecting feelings or expressing them cathartically.

I don't know if I am pleased or worried that so many of the themes in this short book are ones that still preoccupy me and which are present in much of my later writing. These include the importance of body awareness in psychotherapy, the need to help people manage positive as well as negative emotional states, the centrality of early experience, the link between neurobiology and psychoanalysis, the way trauma affects the brain, how neglect affects emotional states differently to abuse, how emotionally charged enactments are central to the therapy process and generally the importance of ensuring that emotions are placed centrally at the heart of the psychotherapeutic practice.

I hope the ideas in this short book do speak to you; they most certainly still have meaning for me.

Graham Music
May 2022

ABOUT THE AUTHOR

Graham Music is a Consultant Child and Adolescent Psychotherapist at the Tavistock Centre in London and an Adult Psychotherapist in private practice. Formerly the Associate Clinical Director of the Tavistock Clinic's Child and Family Department, his passion has always been for working with trauma, and he has spent the last few decades at the Portman Clinic and in the Tavistock's Fostering and Adoption and Kinship Care team.

He has developed and managed a range of services, working with the aftermath of child maltreatment and neglect, and he has prioritized community-based services for people who are often marginalized from mainstream clinic work, including developing services in over 40 schools.

He supervises and teaches a range of training courses in the UK and abroad, delivers keynote conference talks and taught all over the world for a long time.

He has a particular interest in linking cutting-edge developmental findings with therapeutic practice. His publications include *Respark: Igniting Hope and Joy after Trauma and Depression* (2022), *Nurturing Children: From Trauma to Hope* (2019), *Nurturing Natures* (2016, 2010), *Affect and Emotion* (2001), *The Good Life* (2014) and *From Trauma to Harming Others* (co-edited with Ariel Nathanson and Janine Sternberg, 2021).

* * *

Please sign up for Graham Music's newsletter and other information, including blogs, publications and forthcoming events, at https://nurturingnatures.co.uk/sign-up/ or visit his website, nurturingnatures.co.uk. Graham can be contacted by email (gmusic@nurturingnatures.co.uk), on Twitter (https://twitter.com/grahammusic1/) or LinkedIn (www.linkedin.com/in/graham-music-nurturing-natures).

1. INTRODUCTION

The concepts of affect, emotion and feeling and how they relate to psychoanalysis.

This being human is a guest house.
Every morning a new arrival.

A joy, a depression, a meanness,
some momentary awareness comes
As an unexpected visitor.

Welcome and entertain them all!
Even if they're a crowd of sorrows,
who violently sweep your house
empty of its furniture,
still treat each guest honourably.
He may be clearing you out
for some new delight.

The dark thought, the shame, the malice,

meet them at the door laughing,
and invite them in.

Be grateful for whoever comes,
because each has been sent
as a guide from beyond.

—Rumi, The Guest House[1]

In this volume, I make sense of feelings, emotions and affects from a psychotherapeutic, primarily psychoanalytic, perspective. Emotions are central not just to therapy but to all human life. Emotions give signals that we read to make decisions about whether to act in a certain way. If I am tensing and my breathing goes shallow, my body might be signalling danger and, thus, I might run, hide or possibly fight. In other words, emotions are embodied and also have an action tendency.

What is particularly distinctive about a psychoanalytic take on the world of feelings and emotions is two key things.

- Firstly, we are all, to varying degrees, unaware or unconscious of much that motivates us.
- Secondly, there are some things we do not want to feel, and we defend against these. We then experience anxiety when these emotions threaten to break into consciousness.

Such defences can lead to short-term gains ('I don't have to feel a horrible feeling, like pain') but can also lead to longer-term problems because the effort needed to defend against a feeling can lead to living a diminished life. Psychotherapy helps people to become more aware of their non-conscious lives, including repressed or denied emotions, and to develop a capacity to tolerate a wider range of emotional experiences. These twin threads run through the entirety of this short book.

The concepts *feeling, emotion* and *affect* have similar meanings, and psychoanalytic and ordinary dictionaries often define one in relation to the other. Affect is a concept used mainly in academic writing and has a more objective flavour, it is something that can be observed and studied rather than experienced. Its use fits with the traditional distrust of subjective experience in science where, until recently, even in neuroscience, emotion was barely seen as a subject fit for study. Feeling, on the other hand, denotes an internal state, someone's private experience, including sensing of one's emotions. We cannot directly observe feelings, but we can see signs of them, such as an eye tearing up or a leg shaking.

Emotion is the ordinary language equivalent of affect, and both have a more physiological quality than feelings. Affect is often also used to include moods, which are ongoing states, whereas emotions are usually more short-lived. Some people use emotions interchangeably with feelings, but I am sticking to the definition suggested by the neuroscientist Antonio Damasio[2], that emotions are bodily states, which also have action tendencies, whereas feelings are more psychological, internal and private and refer to emotions which are known, processed or made sense of. For example, my heart racing fast might signal an emotional state and, if I am lucky, I might interpret my bodily (emotional) state as a feeling, perhaps as anxiety, or possibly fear or excitement. Unfortunately, the boundaries between the concepts of affect, emotion and feelings are a bit blurry, and I will sometimes use these concepts, especially affect and emotion, interchangeably.

Until a few decades ago, academic psychology separated the study of affect and emotion from cognition and memory, with the latter seen as more appropriate objects of scientific study. In fact, this is an unhelpful distinction. Emotions and cognitions simply cannot be separated, despite what academics have long suggested. Even Freud, when he originally wrote about repressed memories of childhood sexual abuse, described how memories of traumatic events are closely linked with emotions and feelings, something that current neuroscience has borne out, as has recent trauma theory[3]. A memory of abuse, for example, might be in the mind but also shows itself in bodily states and emotional reactions.

Freud believed early in his career that if people discharge emotions which are associated with difficult memories, then these memories lose much of their power. We will see later that this is partly right and partly wrong. Rather than the act of cathartic expression itself being healthy, it is that emotions need to be known, experienced and accepted rather than be defended against. And it is this bearing and experiencing of emotions that is especially curative.

Thus, the cognitive and the emotional seamlessly interweave. For example:

While walking past a school recently, I was reminded of a difficult childhood incident and my feeling of being at school returned, with many of the same anxieties and fears coming back to the surface. Then I felt upset for the young me, then I remembered a friend from that period who had been kind and wondered what happened to him and I thought of a book we both read as adolescents and wondered if I still had it. Then I remembered an anxious dream I used to have and my heart raced ... this all maybe lasted but a few seconds.

Such jumpy trains of associations might be more typical in people like me (possibly with ADHD traits) but they are one of the reason why psychoanalysis has used the technique of free association in which patients are encouraged to say whatever comes to mind. Associations activate other associations, and in such associational trains, we see both thoughts and affects. For example, an emotion, such as fear, might be triggered by a smell (e.g., boiled cabbage reminding me of school dinners) which in turn might evoke a memory of something scary (e.g., being bullied during school lunch breaks) and then all kinds of thoughts and feelings might rush in. Sometimes, this leads to defensive reactions. For example, I might have an anxiety-provoking thought and then start walking fast or eating something, both possible ways of avoiding rather than facing the feelings evoked by the thought.

While it is true that it is hard to separate cognition and emotion, there is one distinction between bodily/emotional memories and those which are more mental which I find very helpful and will unpack as we go along. This is the distinction between what are often called explicit or declarative memories, which are factual, such as remembering the name of a capital city or a date, as opposed to implicit or procedural memories, such as how to do things, which are more embodied memories, including tying a shoelace or driving a car.

This distinction becomes clear when we study people who suffered damage in brain areas linked to specific memories, such as an injury which might lead someone to not be able to recognize their spouse consciously or even remember their name. However, even in these cases, subjects often still act towards their spouses as they did before the injury. This is because elsewhere in the brain, there are circuitries involved in embodied procedural memories, which might not be affected by the damage to areas involved in factual, declarative or explicit memories. Embodied memory systems are needed, for example, to remember things like how to type on a keyboard or to play an instrument, but also to know in our bodies and beings how to be in relationships, and this includes the attachment styles we develop. In therapy, we are generally hoping to understand and often shift such unconscious procedural patterns that are no longer serving us.

A patient of Damasio[4] had calcification in part of her amygdala which meant that she could not feel fear. This might sound like a relief and, if I am honest, I have often wished that I no longer felt fear. In reality, the absence of fear could have terrible consequences. This patient was unable to learn from negative experiences as she did not receive those bodily warning signs that elicit a protective danger response. Imagine not learning that electric fences or fires are dangerous, even after being exposed to them. As Damasio, more than anyone, has made clear: reading emotions, and turning them into feelings, means recognizing and ascribing meaning to body states, such as in the case of pain, a quickened heart rate or a tensing of muscles. In psychoanalytic language, such a process is generally called *containment*. The psychoanalyst Wilfred Bion[5] first used this term, and he described it as transforming what *beta elements* (unprocessed sense impressions) into *alpha function*, a process by which sensations are processed and made sense of, or in Damasio's terms, how emotions are turned into feelings.

As we will see later in more detail, much research[6] shows that emotional experiences, such as trauma, have a profound effect on brain and nervous system functioning, which in turn affects how life is later experienced. A big part of what brains do is make predictions about the immediate future, based on past experiences which we use to interpret cues in the present. Our early learning leads to such predictions, and these predictions often manifest in the form of bodily cues, such as clenching muscles or sweaty palms.

A large body of research, both psychological and neuroscientific, has verified the existence of unconscious, or at least non-conscious, emotional states. For example, people who tend to have avoidant attachment patterns might dismiss the importance of relationships and intimacy or deny, for example, that they need others or to care about closeness with people. Yet when their skin conductance or heart rate is measured when they are asked to recall memories of separation, rejection and threats involving their parents, the results are surprising. The more they use avoidant strategies and deny to themselves or others any discomfort, the more they have strong physiological reactions that signify stress[7]. Their bodies are speaking an emotional truth that their minds are unable to consciously own.

Other fascinating experiments have yielded similar results[8]. For example, some men were given questionnaires which scored their levels of homophobia. They were then shown heterosexual, gay and lesbian pornography while a machine measured what they call 'penile tumescence'[8]. Interestingly, the most vehemently homophobic men had the highest 'penile tumescence' when watching gay male pornography, suggesting that their homophobia was, in part, a powerful denial of their 'real' desires.

It is probable that these men needed to defend against homosexual wishes, which presumably did not fit with their sense of who they felt they should be, and so they resorted to defensive states. As this book proceeds, I will look in more detail at how we cope or do not cope with the different challenges of emotional life and, in that process, how emotions can be denied, defended against, discharged into the body, defensively got rid of or, if we are lucky, embraced and welcomed as Rumi suggested.

2. EARLY EXPERIENCE AND EMOTIONAL STATES

How affects and the capacity for emotional experience develop in infancy and early childhood.

"Do you know who made you?"
"Nobody, as I know on," said the child with a short laugh.
The idea appeared to amuse her considerably; for her eyes twinkled, and she added: —
"I spect I growed. Don't think nobody never made me."
"You find virgin soil there, cousin: put in your own ideas; you won't find many to pull up."
Harriet Beecher Stowe[9]

It has nowadays become widely accepted that our emotional selves are influenced by what we experience when we were young. In recent decades, large bodies of research from related fields such as developmental psychology, neuroscience, attachment theory, psychoanalytic observation of infants and many others, have demonstrated the clear impact of early experiences on development. Genetic endowment is important, but its role relative to that of nurture has been reconsidered in recent years via the new field of epigenetics which aims to describe how genes are turned on or off by different experiences. We might still debate the role of genes, but few now doubt the importance of experiences, especially early ones. Sylvia Plath captured something of this in a poem to her daughter which described her as *'A clean slate with your own face on*'[10].

Thus, while we are born with distinct, genetically-determined predispositions, how and even whether these are turned on is more complicated. I might have a gene that predisposes me to depression or behavioural problems, but with the right sort of parenting, such problems can be avoided. Indeed, experiences of a previous generation, such as trauma, can affect gene expression down to the next generation, and even subsequent ones.

We also now know that *in utero*, high levels of maternal stress shape the endocrine and nervous systems of the unborn child. The human infant is born immature and its brain develops by adapting to whatever environment it finds itself in, to its cultural or emotional world. Their brain, body and nervous system are, in effect, sculpted by their early experiences.

In the early months, the infant depends almost entirely on its mother or primary caretaker for its physical and emotional needs. The infant is born with a brain and nervous system that can regulate important physiological functions such as body temperature and heartbeat. However, the capacity to regulate emotional states comes much later. The infant needs what Freud called a *protective shield* **and** what we might nowadays call an external psychobiological regulator[11] of its emotions, normally the mother or other caregiver. Some describe this process using the metaphor of a mother or parent lending the infant their prefrontal cortex until the infant's own develops.

The infant in distress needs not only to be soothed but also to know that its feelings are understood and that someone is making sense of their experiences for and with them. A 10-month-old baby, Rick, started wailing when, for the first time, he heard the loud sound of the new spin-dryer going at full throttle. His mother, at first, was anxious and worried, wondering what had caused the upset, and had to grapple with her own upset in response to Rick's distress. Soon she realized what had triggered him and picked Rick up and began to carry him around, soothingly letting him know that she understood his distress and that she knew there was no real danger, all conveyed by her touch, posture and tone. She then went back to the machine with him, turning it off and on again several times while talking about what was going on. The words may have made little sense, but the emotional meaning was transmitted through the feeling, rhythm and prosody of her speech. In no time Rick recovered, and the object of terror became an object of interest. Rick soon wanted to turn the machine on and off by himself.

In this interaction, Rick's mother functioned as a

kind of protective emotional shield for Rick, helping him to manage his feelings and interpreting the world for him. Many psychotherapists use such a model of mother-infant interactions to aid them in their practice. Therapeutic interaction has parallels with early parenting processes. Psychotherapists must make sense of feelings in their patients and, in so doing, often also make sense of their own feelings and what is being evoked in them. Infants need another person to modulate their experiences of the world, in fact, we all do, whether as a therapist, friend or partner. Some infants, like some adults, are hypersensitive to external stimuli and more easily shocked by the kind of sudden noises just mentioned. Such hypersensitivity can make the job of being a parent harder, but all infants need adult help to make sense of what they are experiencing.

Infants' capacities are often underestimated. An infant need to only experience something a few times for them to expect the same thing to happen again under similar circumstances. The infant whose cries are ignored or even punished soon learns not to cry when distressed, and learns to ignore their own distress, especially if they have a parent who cannot tolerate such negative feelings. Infants of depressed mothers show depressed behaviour when with non-depressed adults at six months. They learn what to expect and make predictions about likely adult responses.

From early in life, we all form expectations of how interactions are likely to go. As I said, our brains are predictive, we are constantly trying to make sense of the present, based on the past to try to work out what is likely to happen next. These become what Bowlby[12] called internal working models and others have called schemas, or internal object relations or R.I.G.S.

(Representations of Interactions Generalized)[13]. These are partly based on real experience and partly on how our mind interprets these experiences. These expectations tend to become the basis for how we relate to the world in the future. Sometimes we make what are called prediction errors because earlier experiences lead our brains to see and predict what might not be there. For example, I have seen a great many children adopted from traumatic backgrounds who are wrongly fearful of benign and caring adults.

Hilary, a 35-year-old woman, had as a child developed an expectation that she would be rejected if she got angry with her parents, and as an adult she expected to be similarly rebuffed. In relationships, and with her therapist, she was too nice and sugary, assuming that people would reject her if she showed any disgruntlement. This is one example of what is meant by *transference* to someone else, an unconscious transfer of beliefs from a prior relationship onto a current one. Transferences are central to all therapeutic work. When we recognize such patterns, they can start to shift.

Emotions and feelings are very much linked to belief systems. The adopted child who is scared of most adults, and who has come from a family where there was ongoing danger and violence, is not surprisingly transferring early learning onto the present, but in a way that is no longer helping them. They might be fearful of their new adoptive parents, of teachers, be untrusting of adults generally and not believe that anyone can be kind. They perceive the present in terms of past learning, similar to Pavlov's dogs salivating when they hear the bell that signifies the arrival of food. However, in humans such predictions in the brain and body also come with belief systems, feelings and thoughts.

There used to be a big gulf between therapies that focus on internal states, insight and the unconscious, such as psychoanalysis, and more behaviourally-informed therapies. Yet, in recent years, it has been harder to justify these schisms between schools of psychotherapy and psychology because it has become increasingly clear that, in order to work with someone effectively, we need to understand their thoughts, both conscious and unconscious, as well as their feelings, emotions and bodily states; in effect, the whole person. In particular, we can now link our understanding of people's behaviours with their mental states and representations as well as their nervous systems, emotions and feelings.

This brings us back to the distinction mentioned earlier, between declarative and procedural memory. An example of declarative or explicit memory would be remembering facts, such as the name of the capital city of Venezuela. More central to therapeutic work, however, is procedural or implicit memory, our more body-based ways of being. We tend to all have emotional templates of how to be with people, specific ways we expect others to behave with us and how we have learnt to be accepted in relationships. We make unconscious predictions, and we tend to act on them automatically. This might include whether at a party we expect to be liked or shunned, whether when meeting a new person, we tend to be open or closed off, or if we assume people who look a certain way are likely to be dangerous.

Just like a skill such as riding a bicycle, relational learning constitutes a form of procedural memory, something that one learns and then does no more consciously than a centipede consciously thinks about walking. These are deeply ingrained, embodied ways of being. The distinction between procedural and declarative memory is not an absolute one, but it is useful shorthand for thinking about how our emotional lives can form patterns that repeat themselves over time and outside of consciousness. Such patterns are generally laid down when we are very young, often in the first months of life, well before areas of the brain that process factual, declarative memories have developed.

Human infants are rather like barometers of mood states, picking up and responding to the emotional climate created by people around them, sensing clues subtly, learning how it is best to act in their family or culture and working out what is expected. Infants and children in the presence of adults who smile with pleasure often cannot help but smile too, even if they have no idea what the smiling is about. The infant's mood state, and indeed the infant's brain, tends to mirror their parent's face, and, indeed, there is also synchrony between a mother's and infant's brain waves and heartrates. The parent is then a psycho-biological modulator of an infant's experience in the same way a therapist can be to a patient and a friend can be for any of us. Experiences with important adults in early life develop into emotional and brain patterns which can become the default. This applies to learning that distress is not okay to show, to whether it is safe to laugh or explore or to whether adults are dangerous and one must be vigilant and wary.

The first few years of life are when the brain is most sensitive, when it is changing, growing, and adapting, when default ways of being are being laid down and the basis of one's personality is being formed. This, of course, is an argument for aiming to offer help as early as possible, when worrying patterns can still be changed and reversed and newer ones can form. The traumatised child might early on develop a super-highway of neuronal pathways leading to anxiety and hyper-alertness, whereas luckier babies, such as Rick, will develop super-highways to more trusting and easeful emotional responses. If caught early enough, we can develop new healthier pathways and ways of being which can then become our default ones.

Such early templates of emotional experience, as expressed in bodily procedural form, will often become the central focus of therapy. Hilary, the 35-year-old woman mentioned earlier, entered therapy following a series of disappointing relationships in which she felt hurt and rejected. There were clear links between how mistreated she felt by her partners and how she was genuinely mistreated as a child. Not surprisingly, she was also soon mistrustful of her male therapist.

At first, she felt that she had to be nice and sweet with him, but underneath this veneer, more difficult feelings were brewing. She felt that her feelings were ignored, that some of what her partner and her therapist were saying was cruel and rejecting. She insisted, for example, that if her therapist really cared he would see her more often, charge less and be kinder. Such pivotal issues emerged openly in therapy in what we call the *working-through* of issues.

Often, this means both parties in a therapeutic or other relationship experiencing what it is like to be inside an emotional interaction which they both need to understand, allow, make sense of and then actively work their way out of. When we do this, when we allow and consciously get to know the ways in which we might have been pulled into someone's old patterns, then, with time and emotional effort, we can consciously and deliberately work towards not re-enacting such patterns, but rather, with luck, actively find a way to break out of such habitual ways of being. This can feel awkward, even scary, a bit like learning to do something with a non-dominant hand, but that is how emotional patterns change. Hilary needed a therapist who could tolerate the position he was being nudged into and help her to think about the patterns that were being re-enacted inside and outside the consulting room. Insight was needed, and indeed courage too, to see this as a pattern that could be noted, understood and eventually broken. This is a profoundly emotional process for both parties, and not simply about intellectual insight.

Whether we are with partners, friends or therapists, we will inevitably find ourselves prodded unconsciously into re-enacting habitual ways of being. With some people, we are more likely to feel excited or clever or hopeful, and with others anxious or sad or angry. When going to the pub with different friends, I can feel very clever, even gifted on one night, yet I might feel a bit dull or even stupid with another friend the next night. I was of the same intelligence on both nights, but something different is evoked in me by each person. Relational psychoanalysts have helpfully pointed out[14] that to change such patterns, we really must first be prepared to be drawn into them and get to know them intimately from the inside. Only then can we actively, but non-judgmentally and compassionately, help ourselves and others break out of those patterns and build new relational styles and expectations and develop new procedural expectations which can then become new default ways of being. This means being prepared, as therapist or client, to re-experience emotional patterns which often feel like uncomfortable forcefields. As the Michael Rosen poem suggests[15], *'you can't go over it, you can't go under it, you've got to go through it!'*. This can be easier said than done!

3. URGES AND INSTINCTS

Or how Freud first thought about affect, with reference to drive theory, and signal anxiety.

"No arts; no letters; no society; and which is worst of all, continual fear and danger of violent death; and the life of man solitary, poor, nasty, brutish, and short.". Hobbes[16]

Freud himself did not actually write all that much about emotions or feelings. He talked more about drives, by which he meant something akin to instincts and urges. For example, anger or rage were considered by Freud and many of his contemporaries to be linked to an aggressive drive.

There was a different conception of human nature at the time that Freud was writing, one still influenced by the ideas of Thomas Hobbes, of nature being red in tooth and claw[16]. In this view, so-called primitive instincts, such as untrammelled sexual urges and aggressive self-interest, were our primary drives. Freud was of his time, and his theories suggested a culture which worried about 'base' instincts and drives and their destructive power. There was a common notion that these needed to be civilized out, or at least kept at bay.

Feeling sexual desire for the spouse of a friend, or coveting a relatives' possessions, might be something that we are ashamed of feeling and wish we didn't feel. Thus, we might defend against such feelings, possibly denying them to ourselves, or project traits such as inappropriate sexual desire or greed onto others instead of owning them. The moral part of the mind, what Freud called the superego, might censor such desires. But, of course, they still exist, even if we deny their existence to ourselves and others.

Thus, pushing away and denying feelings has costs. Sian, an artist, held an opening of a new exhibition and her eldest daughter, then 19, gave a talk, was witty, insightful, confident and looked particularly beautiful and poised, taking much of the limelight. Sian was proud of her daughter but also noticed a twinge of envy, realizing that the days when she had received such accolades were slipping away. She could not quite enjoy what was supposed to be her big night, instead she forced herself into her role as hostess and was nicer than usual to her daughter. It was only when chatting to friends later in the week that Sian could, with relief and, thankfully, humour, own up to her feelings, such as the loss of her youth, the hopes she had had at that age and the fact that, unlike her daughter, she no longer had her whole future adult life ahead of her.

Psychoanalysis suggests that repressing our real

feelings, whether sexual desires, rivalry or hatred, is counterproductive and costly. This is one reason why psychoanalysis' idea of the 'return of the repressed' has often been associated with the radical challenge to conservative values and mores. Cultural icons such as Elvis Presley in the 1950's, the Sex Pistols in the 1970's and rappers such as Tupac were all feared and championed for endorsing rebellious, sexual and aggressive attitudes that mainstream culture feared and denied. Many early psychoanalysts, such as Wilhelm Reich[17], supported what were genuinely revolutionary sexual, political and educational ideas. In this, the aim was to liberate and free up repressed feelings, especially about sex.

These days, most psychotherapists think that our relationship with repressed and unconscious desires should not be about controlling them, but more about daring to be open to them and embracing what we might otherwise deny. Denial and defences conjure up all kinds of problems. Freud described the issues that arose from sexual repression in Viennese society and the symptoms that could come of it, such as what was then unfortunately termed *hysteria*. Psychoanalysis is both about knowing one's unconscious but also about respecting its awesomeness and not being fearful of it. This quote by H.L. Mencken[18] teases us about how we cannot avoid the unconscious, try as we might!

".... we cease to believe in the unknowable
But there it sits nevertheless
calmly licking its chops."

Sian's jealousy was natural and understandable. Yet many of us can steadfastly deny ever experiencing such emotions. How often do we or people we know deny feelings that are deemed unacceptable? How often do we hear statements like 'I was not angry/jealous/scared/hurt'? It is easy to feel critical of such feelings in others and ashamed of them in ourselves.

Sian probably attempted such an evasion initially when she found herself being nicer than usual to her daughter, probably as an attempt to spare both of them her true feelings. Such a ploy, often done unconsciously, is an example of what Freud called a *reaction formation*, an attempt to deny one's true emotional state by taking on the opposite affect. We see this in people who are said to protest too much, as Shakespeare pointed out long ago. In Emerson's words[19]:

'the louder he talked of his honour the faster we counted our spoons'!

Jealousy, hatred and desire might all be examples of emotions we wish we did not feel, and are typical of unacceptable or denied feelings, urges, drives and emotions.

Most of us would think that Sian's feelings were understandable, and by understandable we might mean that we can sympathise or that her feelings have meanings we can make sense of. This links to another view of emotion as signs to read, almost a form of communication from one part of the self to another. *Signal anxiety* was the concept Freud used to describe this.

If one is in a social situation and one's heart suddenly starts beating fast, we can take this as a sign of something. For example, a young man, Stephen, was at a party, trying to be nice to someone when he realized that his fists were clenching and the muscles in his neck were tightening. He noted he was being tense, even unkind. It was only when noticing this signal that he realized he had been feeling uneasy about feeling pressurized by the person he was talking to. He would rather not have had these feelings of dislike or unease; he liked to think of himself as a 'nice person' and so did not want to acknowledge what he was feeling. Hence, he was still trying to be nice and friendly. However, when he owned his real feelings in therapy later, rather than deny them, and realised that such feelings were in fact appropriate, he felt relief and his body relaxed.

Possibly, in my earlier example, Sian's feelings about her daughter were a message to her. She had not yet managed to face painful feelings about her move into middle age. Banishing feelings as opposed to daring to face them may help to avoid a painful experience in the moment, but these feelings and their effects remain there, 'licking their chops'. Defending against feelings is costly, often giving rise to a range of symptoms. In Sian's case, her denial was making her tense and brittle, but was also preventing her from confronting what it means to be getting older and embarking on the next phase of life. Her defences against those feelings included manically throwing herself into work and being unable to remain still, which was also having an effect on her sleep and health. Stephen's defences were leading him to be tense and irritable and turn to drinking and other negative habits.

Following Damasio, our bodily emotional responses can be thought of as signs which we can learn to decipher, a skill called *interception*. Some emotional states are not welcomed, in fact, are avoided, shunned even, and can seem like an alien presence that has shockingly taken us over. This sense of 'otherness', of feelings being 'out of character', might be like Freud's conception of instinctual drives over which we feel we have no power. Psychoanalysis teaches us to respect the surprises that can be sprung upon us by the unconscious, even if we do not like them.

Stephen, the young man at the party, had been going through a hard time, including pressure at work, and this had led him to be more aggressive and reactive than usual. He could not separate an appropriate response to the person who was pressuring him and how he was feeling generally; he could not read his own signs easily and so he tried to override them. Afterwards, he was shocked at himself and said, 'It was not like me'. This statement was unpacked in therapy where he also remembered other times when he had felt out of control, particularly in hormonally induced, powerful emotional states during adolescence.

Whether it is still helpful to think in terms of drives is controversial these days, but, certainly, we can all be confronted by passions and overwhelming feelings that we struggle to manage, feelings we might wish could be get rid of. In fact, psychotherapists, as well as mindfulness practitioners, tend to believe that it is much better to try to help people accept, manage or integrate these frightening emotional states than it is to get rid of them. It is better to try to accept and bear rather than fight. The fighting of unwanted feelings often means that they keep popping up anyway in a 'whack-a-mole' fashion. In addition, fighting our feelings requires energy and effort and gives rise to tension, which has its own costs. The philosopher Martin Buber quoted a sage[20] saying that God created man "*not to be caged by his lusts but to be free in them."* Psychotherapy, like mindfulness, suggests we learn to live with emotional states, to 'fold them into' our experience or to contain them, so that we can accept them as 'welcome guests', in Rumi's words[21].

4. MANAGING LOSS

Mourning as a typical example of emotional pain and defences against it.

Suppressed grief suffocates, it rages within the breast, and is forced to multiply its strength.
Attributed to Ovid

Mourning, and managing loss, are subjects that teach us much about emotional life, and, therefore, it was one of the first areas of affective experience that psychoanalysis grappled with. Freud described how profound losses can give rise to what was then called melancholia and which we would now see as a serious form of depression. Both in depression and bereavement, people often withdraw from the world, can seem lacklustre, be self-critical, morbidly preoccupied with events of the past and feel very low. Freud suggested that we would probably consider someone struggling with ordinary bereavement symptoms to be psychiatrically ill if we did not know the true cause of their behaviour. For many, mourning and managing loss is a transitory process, but some people can get stuck, and even addicted, to their feelings. Another sage said,

"There are two kinds of sorrow ...When a man broods over the misfortunes that have come upon him, when he cowers in a corner and despairs of help, that is a bad kind of sorrow ...The other kind of sorrow is the honest grief of a man whose house has burned down, who feels his need deep in his soul and begins to build anew.'[20]

Marion, a 45-year-old mother, had been married to Peter for 18 years when he suddenly died of a heart attack. Marion was, at first, in a state of shock and numbness. She could not take in the awful truth of what had happened and, for a long time, she was in denial. For example, she was preparing Peter's evening meal as usual, unable to take in the unbearable reality of his death. Sometime later, she began to feel terribly guilty and wondered what she could have done to prevent his death. She then also found herself feeling furious with Peter, berating him that now she had to work so hard, that he was selfish to leave their family in this way.

Marion felt ashamed of her rollercoaster of feelings but, in fact, everything she experienced is common across the process of bereavement. Her feelings would ebb and flow as she moved in and out of numbed disbelief, irrational clinging to the past, a furious rage with Peter, dreadful heart-rending pain, self-hating guilt and more. For a long time, she seemed to withdraw into her own world, barely available even to her children.

Those who have suffered tragic life events such as this know that it can take a long time to recover. Vera Britten[22] wrote poignantly of the death of her lover that 'time, they told me, with maddening uniformity, would heal. I resented the suggestion bitterly...clinging assiduously to my pain I did not know then that if the living are to be of any use in this world, they must always break faith with the dead'.

It is a long painful journey to work through loss and to find a way to move back into life, hopefully, eventually finding a sense of gratitude for lost loved ones. Such losses often continue to reverberate throughout one's life.

Some, unfortunately, do not manage to ever work through such lifechanging events. An example from literature is Miss Haversham in Dickens's Great Expectations[23]. She was jilted on her wedding day and lived until old age stuck in a time warp, surrounded externally by a decaying wedding cake, cobwebbed furniture and a clock stopped at the hour of her betrayal. Internally, she was as eaten up as her mice-ridden wedding cake, full of hatred and bitterness and fantasies of revenge. She is a stark example of the costs of not being able to work through a painful loss and the process of mourning, in time to move back into life.

We all constantly face losses in life. Indeed, life is made up of constant loss, from giving up the breast as an infant and the death of a beloved pet to fundamental life changes such as leaving school, moving house, a child outgrowing its home or the death of a loved one. Some of us manage these better than others, and this is linked to our capacity to process and bear emotional experiences. In the last section, we met Sian who we saw struggling with her daughter's move into womanhood and her own transition to middle age. The move to middle age marks one kind of loss, signalling the end of youth and a step towards frailty and death. These are painful things to confront and face, and some cope by denial, possibly wearing clothes more suitable to younger people or rushing headlong into frenetic activity, overworking, affairs or addictive activities.

The school leaver who scornfully denigrates younger school pupils, who desperately tries to take on the role of a young adult, may also in part be trying to ward off painful feelings about the loss of the safe and known, of needed adults, secure routines and family life. The cliché of the man who tries to deny his middle age by buying sports cars exemplifies a wish to avoid the brutal facts of mortality and the failing body. Emotions felt in such circumstances, such as excitement, elation or triumph, can be used to ward off or defend against more painful ones. One affective state can be used to fend off another; of course, some of us use sadness to ward off rage we fear while others use anger to ward off a sadness they cannot bear.

Psychoanalysis has traditionally argued that the emotional pain that life throws at us cannot be evaded without cost, that defences against feelings have consequences, but that when emotions are faced and borne, we generally feel more alive and life becomes all the richer for it. There can be tremendous relief when we embrace life, including difficult feelings when they are managed and not evaded. The great psychoanalysts Donald Winnicott was hinting at this when he apparently said, 'oh god, may I be alive when I die'. The relief when resistance is let go of, such as when a fought-against sadness eventually gives way to tears, is typical. I saw this recently with an angry, frantic child whose beloved grandmother had died, and, at last, let out an outpouring of grief that everyone but they themselves knew had been inside them all along.

Central to emotional maturity is learning to tolerate and face unpleasant realities. Most contemporary psychoanalytic theorists would argue that people are helped by something inside themselves, an unconscious part of their personality that is often called a good *internal object*, a kind of guiding inner voice that helps us to manage emotional challenges. Such capacities are often viewed as something alive, like a helpful figure, one that can look after us when we need help.

In some people, such psychological capacities may never develop, possibly because their emotional lives were never taken seriously when young. In such cases, the job of the psychotherapist is not just that of the bereavement counsellor, of allowing a natural process of grief or mourning to unfold. Rather, it can be more like helping a young child, now as an adult, to sympathetically and painstakingly develop the very equipment which allows the rest of us to experience, tolerate and make sense of our emotional lives.

Bion called this equipment a *container*, containment being that capacity to take in another's emotional experience, modulate and process it and then digest it. If we can do this for and with another person, we can give a version of this now safe, processed and detoxified emotion back to them in a form that allows them to bear and manage it themselves. Central to being a good parent or therapist is developing such a capacity for capacious containment which again allows people to stay with and not defend against feelings such as of loss. Loss, like death, is inevitable and part of the fabric of life. Emotional maturity, to the extent that it exists, means being able to contain, stay with and manage such difficulties, including losses large and small, from losing cherished objects to a child leaving home to the end of relationships to losing our health and of course, our very lives.

5. NEGLECT

How being emotionally neglected leads to neglecting one's own and others' emotions.

... Child! I see thee! Child I've found thee!
Midst of the quiet all around thee!
Child I see thee! Childe I spy thee
And thy mother sweet is nigh thee!-
Child I know thee! Child no more ...
Keats[24]

To know we are experiencing a feeling, we need to have had the experience of our emotional signals being understood and made sense of. We saw an example of this with baby Rick, described earlier, who experienced the physical response of shock to the sudden loud noise of the spin-dryer. When his mother noticed this and helped him to re-regulate and realise that this was not dangerous, he not only calmed down, but some sense of this experience was created. I might have a bodily reaction, like tensing and an increasing heart rate, but this does not really become what we can call a 'feeling' unless we have the equipment to make sense of the bodily reaction. We might assume that Rick was frightened, but in fact he did not yet know that he was experiencing what we call fear. However, as he and any of us gain and make sense of more of such states, we learn to trust that we can know what our emotions are.

Some children do not get this kind of input and so their capacity simply does not develop. We see this especially in children and adults who have suffered emotional neglect. By neglect I mean that their emotional lives were not taken seriously. There are gradations of this, from the extreme end of the scale, such as children left in depriving orphanages, to the less extreme end, where a parent simply cannot bear to be in touch with feelings, their own or other's. Either way, the carefully attuned acknowledgment and kind attention to emotional states is lacking, and if this is ongoing and consistent, then a child will not develop the capacity to recognise their own emotional states. As a result, they might become emotionally blunted or numbed.

Emotional neglect is not always easy to spot. In children, we are quicker to act when seeing overt abuse such as bruises or parental drug use or violence than neglect. It is not always clear what is a neglectful experience, particularly as neglect is the absence of something rather than its presence. In extreme cases though, this lack of basic emotional nurturing leads to serious psychological, emotional and physical delays as the pioneering studies of institutional life by Spitz[25] in the 1940s showed. Spitz filmed infants in institutional settings who displayed excruciating behaviours, witnessing staring into space, rocking, turning from side to side and lying still for long periods with glazed expressions. They had given up any hope of human contact and had withdrawn into a self-contained world, becoming very hard to reach.

It is hard to imagine what the moment-to-moment life is like of a child abandoned in a neglectful orphanage, what the lack of physical contact may feel like, let alone the lack of anyone knowing or being interested in what you are feeling or thinking. In experiencing emotional neglect, children simply do not have a parent or other adult who is sensitive to their bodily and emotional states, who psychologically holds and contains them and who is attuned to their gestures and experiences. Thus, they stay out of touch with their emotions, or rather never get to know them. It is like having a muscle that is never used and consequently withers away. They will neither experience that mutual wide-eyed delight so often seen between infants and their parents nor get to know or expect others to understand their emotional worlds or experience the help needed to navigate anxious or frightening moments. The experiences that normally help build emotional intelligence and confidence are generally lacking in severely neglected people who often live in a flat and desultory world.

Ironically, it can be a challenge to remain psychologically alert and interested in people who are emotionally dulled down. In therapy sessions with people who have suffered neglect, both children and adults, our minds can wander. Their bodily responses give the needed clues: a dullness, listlessness, lack of feeling. As research shows,[28] neglected people have less ability to understand emotional expressions. Tragically, they also experience little pleasure, including in human contact, and so are less likely to inspire hope, affection or enjoyment in those around them.

Many of the emotionally neglected children and adults I have worked with have not developed a belief that they can be of interest to other people, and they have long ago stopped trying to get attention from others. In the worst cases, they can seem uninterested in anything at all, lacking curiosity, hope and expectations. I can remember how time seemed to pass really slowly with one orphanage-reared child. Perhaps this is not a coincidence as time passing excruciatingly slowly was probably what his life had felt like at the orphanage and why he and other similar children and adults engaged in numbing rituals. Yet, with such people I knew that to make a difference, I needed to find some spark of liveliness in myself to use in our work together.

What I am here describing is a form of emotional *resonance* and what in psychoanalysis we think of as our *countertransference*. We used to think that our own responses to others were what we call *projections*, one person getting rid of feelings into another, an idea I will discuss later. However, we now know that as a very resonant species, this is often a sign of how humans tend to subtly pick up emotional states from other people. And, in a bodily resonating way, that the emotional states of others have an almost contagious effect on us and our own nervous systems and states of mind.

It is worth stressing that the neglected people I describe have often not suffered overt trauma, such as being beaten or sexually abused or witnessing violence.

More important than bad things that happened to them is what did not happen to them, omission rather than commission, the lack of good experiences that foster healthy emotional development. The lethargy or lack of enthusiasm one can feel with people who have not properly come alive is very different from how we might feel around violent, edgy offenders or traumatised, abused children who can be aggressive and reactive, and with whom I certainly am often on edge and anxious, but emotionally present.

Thus, many neglected people can attract too little attention. The patient I mentioned above, who had been at an orphanage, was too often described as 'good' and 'quiet' in school; a description often heard with such worrying presentations of the self. Physically, he reached the usual milestones, but he demanded little emotionally from others and received little in return. This became a kind of feedback loop. Having been starved of good attention early on, he emitted only subtle, faint, too easily missed signals of desire for interaction. He certainly had no response when anyone asked what he was feeling, he simply did not know, drew a blank and, indeed, probably felt blank. What he needed most was for the adults in his life, his adoptive parents and his teachers, to help him to understand how and why he had turned out the way he had, and then to help him become more alive, hopeful and emotionally present to himself and others.

In his case, we had to help his parents to translate seemingly purely physiological gestures, such as his legs jiggling or him clenching his fists, into the language of emotions ('ooh, you seem worried about that nice big dog' or 'ouch, that was a big loud noise'). Having his feelings understood allowed him to experience relief and led to him calming and then to showing interest. Such a simple, emotionally empathic, resonant response, in fact, is another example of containment, in Bion's language, a turning of beta elements into alpha function. Such an ability to read bodily signals and learn their significance is crucial for emotional development. If my heart races, it might mean that I am anxious or possibly excited, and I can learn the difference, but first I must learn to recognise that my heart is racing and that this might have significance.

Early neglect has profound effects on brain growth[36] and leads to impairment in cognitive and language abilities, social and communication skills and problems with emotional regulation. Generally, the more severe the deprivation, the worse the effects. The good news is that if we intervene early enough, we can make a big difference. The longstanding Bucharest Intervention Study[27] found that orphanage children placed in good family care early enough lost many of their symptoms, including ritualistic rocking, they developed better social skills and, most excitingly, researchers saw hopeful brain changes, such as growth in white matter[28], signifying that, if caught early on, many of these effects can be reversed.

People who have been highly neglected are often passive and listless and can show little desire to interact with peers or caregivers. They are not surprisingly less able to recognise facial cues[29] and often seem uninterested in emotional worlds. I have emphasised how recognising emotional states means recognising emotional signals in the body. Those who cannot manage this have often been given the label of *alexithymic*, a condition marked by a cut-offness from emotions.

The psychoanalyst Joyce McDougall worked a lot with people who she described as *normopathic*, by which she meant they seemed somewhat dull, what we might think of as overly normal and who, in truth, were often uninteresting as well as uninterested. She found that many had psychosomatic issues too, which makes sense if we think that emotional issues which are not understood or even known can reside in the body instead. McDougal, like many researchers and psychoanalysts, found that such people often had a paucity of imagination as well, a lack of creativity alongside low levels of emotional aliveness.

What has shifted in psychoanalytic and therapeutic understandings since Freud's day is a realization that such states can be caused by a lack of development, a lack of an attuned and empathic parent who gives the kind of input which gives rise to an emotional containing capacity. Originally, psychoanalysis assumed that it was psychological overwhelm, such as a trauma, or psychological conflict, that shuts down emotional awareness. However, in the cases of neglect I have been discussing here, what we see is not a shutting-down of functions so much as a lack of such capacities ever developing, a lack of the growth of an emotionally aware mind able to know about or be interested in feelings.

6. TRAUMA

How overwhelming experiences kill off emotional capacities.

The first Day's Night had come –
And grateful that a thing
So terrible –had been endured –
I told my Soul to sing –

She said her Strings were snapt –
Her Bow –to Atoms blown –
And so to mend her –gave me work
Until another Morn –
Emily Dickinson [30]

Trauma was originally a medical term referring to a serious wound or injury. A wound, like a head injury, pierces an outer membrane such as the skin that protects the physiological system underneath. An emotional trauma is somewhat similar; a working definition of a traumatic experience might be that trauma overwhelms one's usual emotional protective layers. The starkest examples are the most unthinkable ones, such as surviving the holocaust or being a victim of torture. The unthinkability of such experiences is often a sign of their traumatic nature, as those experiences break through any layer of protection and become too difficult to process. Indeed, the parts of the brain involved in thinking often go offline during trauma. While I have in this book been focusing on the importance of developing the capacities to process emotional experiences instead of denying them, genuinely traumatic experiences can be too difficult to tolerate or process.

Trauma always has a profound effect on emotional lives and capacities, but more so if it is ongoing developmental trauma in early life rather than a one-off trauma later in life. Trauma can lead to a variety of emotional reactions. In some, it can lead to a heightened emotional reactivity as seen in certain personality disorders. In more severe cases, it can lead to serious emotional shut-down, even dissociative states, a numbing of emotional aliveness.

What is traumatic for one person might well be less so for another. For example, children who have been abused are more likely to make a better recovery if they have also had good early emotional experiences to compensate. The seriousness of the abuse is a big factor, though not necessarily the main one. It is their emotional capacities and experiences from before the abuse, and the help they received in processing the experiences, that counts almost as much as the severity of the abuse.

Some experiences, of course, such as having been held in a concentration camp, would overwhelm just about anyone, although even in such a situation, some have better capacities to survive than others as Viktor Frankl graphically described[31]. Our early experiences, the kind of parenting we receive, as well as factors such as the relative unsafeness of our current environment, trauma, poverty and danger, all impact on the extent to which we develop capacious capacities for emotional containment, and thus for withstanding trauma. We all have differently thick or thin skin, learn to tolerate different thresholds of emotional input and will be thrown off balance by different experiences. A good experience of containment, in Bion's sense, helps people to develop an emotional skin or membrane that is not too porous, nor too rigid. This leads to emotional openness and flexibility and a trust that one can bear and 'roll with' challenging times.

Trauma is almost, by definition, overwhelming and, hence, often leads to high stress levels, difficulty focusing and concentrating and problems with both knowing and regulating emotions. It often comes with a hyper alertness that can make it difficult to relax and can give rise to all kinds of interpersonal difficulties. Victims of abuse, especially children with no safe adult to rely on, often resort to desperate measures to survive. Some are highly reactive, many identify with their abusive caregiver and become violent, while others survive through dissociation, an extreme form of psychic numbing often seen after trauma.

Traumatised people who are later exposed to frightening images show extreme arousal in brain regions such as the amygdala and a deactivation of the prefrontal regions necessary for self-reflection, empathy and emotional regulation[32]. If the trauma or abuse starts early, then a child's repertoire to deal with such affronts is even more limited.

Children and adults who have been subjected to trauma and abuse are generally not able to use their emotional bodily reactions for effective guidance about what is or is not safe. Their bodies can become geared to acting fast to avoid danger. This is a useful survival reaction in the face of immediate threat, but one that, when overly relied on, does not help in ordinary social interactions. The nuanced awareness of emotional life, what has been called the granularity of experience, can get turned off in a person whose primary focus has been survival and avoiding danger and threat.

Gerry was typical in these respects. He was born into a violent home with a chaotic, drug-using mother, unsafe adults and much aggression. He was already extremely jumpy and ill-at-ease as a four-year-old, reacting to things aggressively that passed other children by, getting into fights and barely being able to be still or concentrate. His brain, body and nervous system were geared up to manage danger and threat. When placed in foster care, he could not feel safe, trust or calm down. His deep-seated beliefs that adults were dangerous would take years to unlearn, alongside therapy for his family and psychoeducation for his teachers.

Gerry had experienced the most damaging form of trauma, which is interpersonal trauma. And worse, trauma from those who should have been protecting him from danger. Such early complex trauma is far more likely than other traumas, such as car accidents, to give rise to Post Traumatic Stress Disorder (PTSD) symptoms. Maybe the worst form of interpersonal trauma is that inflicted by a child's carers. When a carer turns abuser, a child's whole world becomes unsafe and unpredictable. Serious abuse often leads to fear, helplessness, shame, rage, betrayal and resignation. Not surprisingly, many children who have been maltreated are seen as 'problematic' in school and elsewhere and become oppositional and aggressive. Stimuli such as the loud voice of a teacher, the stare of a peer or the humiliation of not understanding something can instantly trigger disturbed behaviour. They can quickly see threat where there is none, leading to an escalation of challenging behaviour.

Trauma can, thus, impair the ability to manage everyday life, in particular impacting on the capacity to benefit from relationships with others, whether adults or peers. Traumatized people can often come to believe deep down, in their bodies and nervous systems, that it is not safe to be vulnerable, to trust or to rely on anyone. They often tragically reject the help that they so badly need, a phenomenon the child psychotherapist Henry described as double-deprivation[33]. We know that such children are often less able to be in touch with their own distress and are unlikely to have sympathy for other upset children.

This makes even more sense because the worst trauma is often that which is perpetrated by the very people who should be providing solace and care. Both traumatised children and adults often cope with their very unpredictable and complicated early lives by flipping between being very reactive and edgy, but often also by developing a controlling strategy as a desperate attempt to predict a volatile world.

We often get clues about this in dreams and fantasies or, in the case of children, in their play. Both reveal how such people, whether children or adults, live in mental worlds that are frightening, chaotic and unpredictable. In their stories and play, these children tend to enact scenes in which adults are untrustworthy, violent and, indeed, horribly cruel. The minds of these children can be filled with dangerous and frightening thoughts, disasters and tragedies, and a belief that the world is unsafe and unpredictable[34].

In trauma, then, our emotional membrane is pierced, we lack a sense of safety and we need to resort to more survival-based modes of being. In trauma, parts of the brain necessary for processing emotional experience, for empathy, for autobiographical narrative and for emotional regulation, are all online comparatively less. This is an appropriate immediate response to a life-threatening danger, such as being faced with a predator or violent human, when survival responses trump the need for emotional regulation, empathy or subtle interoception. Survival in such a situation absolutely requires hyper-awareness of threat and danger. The cost of this, though, can be the lack of developing a more nuanced understanding of one's own and other people's feeling states.

In people who have suffered ongoing developmental trauma at the hands of those who should have been looking after them, as opposed to one-off trauma, there is little space for recovery, for development of an internal sense of safeness and ease, what we have called a good internal object. In such cases, it is far less likely for them to take in attuned, reflective attention from another, the kind which facilitates emotional understanding of the self and other. Instead, trauma often gives rise to hypervigilance and controlling behaviours, an overalertness to danger, a profound lack of ease and a much less nuanced ability to bear, process and manage emotional experience generally.

7. CUT OFF FROM FEELINGS

About people who have little capacity for emotional life.

The body's life is the life of sensations and emotions. The body feels real hunger, real thirst, real joy in the sun or the snow, real pleasures in the smell of roses or the look of a lilac bush; real anger, real horror, real love, real tenderness, real warmth, real passion, real hate, real grief. All the emotions belong to the body and are only recognized by the mind.
D.H. Lawrence[35]

As D.H. Lawrence suggested, emotions are rooted in the body. The ones he describes, passion, tenderness, warmth, even grief and hate, all make life much richer when experienced fully. However, for all of us at times, and for many people too much of the time, certain feelings seem unmanageable, best avoided and pushed away, denied and never felt.

The human mind and nervous system have developed ingenious ways of avoiding what seems unbearable. For example, a common response to terrible news is numbness or disbelief, and a traumatized person may cope by dissociating or going off into his or her own world. The abused girl may need to dispel thoughts about the unthinkable nature of her predicament by denying the awfulness of what she has experienced, and in some situations, even dissociate by leaving her body during abusive episodes.

Similarly, it is generally foolhardy for the young boy who gets beaten by his parents to protest, as his protests might lead him to be punished further, and such a child may ignore or forget his unhappiness or anger. Few would deny the sensibleness of these ways of cutting off emotional experience. We now know how it is not necessarily helpful to put people in touch with painful feelings prematurely. The rapid dispatching of busloads of counsellors to the aftermath of traumatic events has been challenged for good reason. It is not always the right time to stare pain in the face, and sometimes people need help to forget rather than to remember. As Brian Keenan[36] wrote following his imprisonment and torture in Beirut, '*to drag a man into talking of something he has neither the desire nor the ability to discuss is a kind of selfish brutality.*'

However, there can be costs to becoming out of touch with feelings and unaware of bodily signals of emotions. In a group on a course I ran, Marcia, James and Frank were talking about the pressures of the syllabus. Then, Frank talked about being angry with the course leaders for being less present and how this reminded him of his father's treatment of him, how when he was young his father was often absent. He then told us how sometimes sad feelings could well up inside him when he was with his own young son. Marcia said that she felt the same, but also felt guilty that she sometimes just wanted to get away from her children and could not bear to spend too much time with them. James had joined in earlier conversations about the pressures of the course, but in the presence of Frank's upset and Marcia's anger he began to look awkward, started fidgeting and eventually made an excuse to get up to leave. We might wonder what was going on for James, who had a 'laddish' tough demeanour, but often headed for an escape route when emotional matters were being discussed. We would probably say that he was threatened by such issues, that he defended against his feelings, that he could not handle them and also that he was not conscious of his responses.

Our culture has moved away a little, but perhaps nowhere near far enough, from cultural tropes of a masculinity based on being strong but unfeeling, symbolized by tough icons of my childhood like John Wayne or Clint Eastwood, who both took on roles of hard men of few words. Eastwood often played supernatural characters returned from the dead, literally non-human, and, hence, non-feeling. In *Hang 'Em High*, a sheriff tells him to go to hell and he replies, 'I've already been there'. This is an idealization of a tough, thick-skinned and uncommunicative person whose emotions are deliberately locked well away[37]. These are powerful defences that, unfortunately, are still often culturally sanctioned.

James' veneer was less tough than that of such

characters, he lacked Eastwood's laconic confidence, but he had little capacity to know his own emotional experience. He had had a troubled adolescence, including a period of anorexia. Yet at the time he did not feel that anything was wrong and, in fact, appeared not to know what others meant when they used emotional words like 'sad' or 'annoyed'. James was later given a diagnosis of autism and he felt great relief to learn this and to meet with others who experienced the world in the way he did. James was, of course, not feelingless, but rather felt things too much, he was overwhelmed by feelings, and indeed by sensations, and it was this feeling of being overwhelmed which led him to look for an escape route.

Most of us can manage feelings better than others. Some might be quick to let other people (and themselves) know when they are happy but cannot admit when they are sad, and others are quick to know anger but cannot admit to vulnerability. Still others have a finely-honed sensibility to the world of emotions, a capacity for emotional granularity, able to differentiate the subtlest nuances between states such as anger, irritation, annoyance or between feeling peeved as opposed to disconcerted as opposed to uptight or rankled or vexed.

This is partly cultural. Most cultures have their own unique concepts not seen in others, and this leads to the world being experienced differently. Some cultures lack, for example, a conception of guilt as opposed to shame and so some might struggle to explain what we might call guilt. The Japanese have a concept, *amae*, which is not really translatable into Western languages but loosely describes an expectation of being loved and cared for, while the Danish concept of *hygge* is equally hard to translate, but refers to being in part a warm, cosy relationship with others. Our language and culture frame our experiences of the world. As Eva Hoffman wrote in her book Lost in Translation,[38] *'Sometimes, when I find a new expression, I roll it on the tongue, as if shaping it in my mouth gave birth to a new shape in the world.'*

Each family too can be said to have their own emotional culture. In some families, rage is frowned upon, but sadness is allowed, while in others worry is more acceptable than exuberance. Someone growing up in a home where jealousy was stigmatized might work hard to avoid admitting being jealous and to disguise this feeling from themselves and others. Such a person might be seen to slam a door a little too loudly when their wife was talking to someone else, but might not actually know that they are jealous, or in other words, they cannot own their own feelings.

James' hasty retreat from the emotionally-laden conversation is common in people who feel profoundly uncomfortable when in contact with feelings in themselves or others. The caricature of a man who spends all his time on his computer or the female academic who immerses herself in the world of books and the intellect, both of whom might struggle to manage real relationships, are examples of this predicament. Psychoanalysis has traditionally used the term *schizoid* for people who are seen as somewhat detached and defended against emotions. This is an exaggerated version of something we all know, such as reaching for a screen, cigarette, chocolate bar or some other distraction rather than face some unsettling feeling.

Certainly, we can all defend against feelings which

we feel we cannot bear or manage. Yet, I often find it more helpful to think about this as not just defending against feelings, but as having the capacity and psychic equipment to open up to emotions and transform them into bearable feelings.

Earlier I mentioned how emotions can function as bodily signals from one part of the self to another. Someone who has been tense and edgy and has a headache and then feels deep relief and ease when their partner returns from a trip, might only then realize how much they missed and need their partner. Others may not be able to make this connection and may not recognize their initial tension or later relief.

In experiments with infants aged about one year old, their mothers are asked to suddenly leave the room. In response, some infants cry and get very upset while others barely react and just carry on as if nothing had happened. These latter children, often labelled as having an avoidant attachment relationship, also seem not to notice when their mothers return, whereas the securely attached infants rush to their mothers for comfort. Yet when the heart rates, adrenalin and cortisol levels of both groups are measured, they all have similar physiological reactions to their mother's disappearance.

Behaviours alone could not reveal this. Those in avoidant attachment relationships are clearly less in touch with their own bodily cues, so, in effect, could not recognise emotional/bodily distress signals which would allow them to have a feeling we might call upset. These are generally people whose parents could not bear their child's upset, and such children learn young to cut off such signals in themselves and others. As a consequence, they are far more likely to grow up less emotionally literate, less able to talk about feelings and less likely to form loving, physically and emotionally close bonds.

There are adults who function perfectly well in this way, who can seem to live normal lives, some might think too normal. These might include those about whom, as I described earlier, the psychoanalyst Joyce McDougall coined the term *normopaths*[39] and who the psychoanalyst Christopher Bollas[40] described as having *normotic* personalities. Yet they have developed their traits, like all of us, for understandable reasons, as a way of adapting to their family's culture and expectations. They generally lived in families where feelings were not 'done', where being 'held in mind' and empathized with were low on the agenda. Such people do not always find their way to psychotherapy, but when they do, the task for a long time is often to help them start to notice emotional signals, often initially in the body, such as a tensing of muscles or a rawness in the chest, and then to start to make connections between such bodily cues and what we might call feelings.

Thankfully, there are no templates for emotional health and the world is made up of a multitude of different personality types, the majority of whom can live lives which mostly feel good and which allow them to contribute to society. We do not need a subtle or nuanced understanding of emotions to do everything that is valuable, whether computer programming, engineering, being a bomb disposal expert or a surgeon. We cannot or should not try to mould anyone into a therapist's or society's idea of emotional health, but we can nonetheless remember that there are costs as well as gains to developing a personality based on not feeling feelings.

8. FLOODED BY FEELINGS

Catharsis, emotional flooding and the idea that it is best to get feelings out.

'It makes me want to scream ....may I? .... Because that's maybe what I need most of all, to howl, a pure howl, without any words between me and it! .....
Philp Roth, *Portnoy's Complaint*[41]

While defending against, or not having feelings at all, has costs, this does not mean that it is always healthier or better to express them and 'get them out', as some assume. Ray brought his son to a child guidance clinic, complaining that he was out of control and always getting into trouble. In describing his son's emotional state, he said that 'he has too much anger inside and he needs to let it out'. The idea that we may have feelings inside which we need to get rid of is a commonly held belief, based on a view of emotions as being like bodily substances that we need to discharge. This is a kind of toxic waste model of emotionality, in which the bad feelings will do us or someone else harm if allowed to remain inside. Freud's earliest therapeutic methods placed an emphasis on what was then called *abreaction* or *catharsis*, and he found that symptoms did improve, albeit often only temporarily, when patients could experience and express previously repressed or denied feelings.

This idea intuitively makes sense. Ruby told me how she was tense and stressed whenever her husband came home. She rushed around, determinedly setting about household tasks, but her whole body and musculature was taut, like a sprung coil. She explained how, when the phone rung, and it was a concerned friend, her manner was brusque and abrasive, brushing aside her friend's kind interest. She had been like this for a few days, and her husband was concerned and perplexed. She had also been keeping him at bay, but when he presented her with a bunch of flowers, her manner softened and she was surprised to find herself sobbing as she allowed herself to be comforted. As she relaxed, she realized what had been going on. The flowers were what he knew to be her favourite chrysanthemums, her favourites because her father would bring them home to her mother every Friday, the happiest time of the week for her. On seeing the flowers, she felt a sudden and overwhelming longing for her father and realized that they were approaching the anniversary of her father's death.

From one angle, we might say that she was carrying around feelings which she was able to 'let out' upon her husband's return. Another way of looking at this is that her husband helped her to manage and process feelings that she was warding off. Rather than getting rid of her feelings, she was helped to have them. There are many forms of therapy, ranging from *gestalt* to encounter groups, which stress the need to express one's feelings, and it is the expression of emotionality which therapists have often deemed therapeutic. Psychoanalysis would come at this from a slightly different angle and consider the capacity for emotional processing to be central. Sometimes, we need help in bearing and tolerating emotional experiences, something a mother often does for a child, and a friend, spouse or therapist might do for us. The value of expressing feelings is not in just getting them out but in learning to bear them. Humans are not pressure cookers and getting something off our chest does not mean our feelings just fly into the ether and eviscerate. What is helpful is having someone, or a part of the self, who can bear an emotional state. And through experiences of this, the very equipment for processing emotional states is forming, equipment which Bion described as a container.

In another example, a young child, Jessica, was angrily crashing around in her bedroom. Her mother came near her and said, 'yes, I understand Jessica, you are very, very cross, it just doesn't feel fair that Martha (her sister) has gone out.' At this, Jessica surprisingly calmed down and was able to talk about being upset that she could not go with her sister. And then, Jessica could be sad for a while and eventually eat her supper.

The crashing around was not about expressing and getting rid of feelings so much as about acting out unprocessed emotions. She felt better not when her emotions were expressed in a cathartic way, but rather when her feelings were expressed but also made sense of, in effect detoxified and made bearable.

Hopefully, in time, we all develop some capacity to do this for ourselves, although most of us might always need friends, partners or others to help us get there. Such a capacity for emotional reflection and regulation normally develops via the kind of parenting we receive, but can also be changed by experiences later in life, such as therapy. Thus, expressing feelings, getting rid of or evacuating them can be important but is often not sufficient. What we need is to have our emotions understood and processed, either by another person, such as a parent or therapist, or, in time, by the self.

Some people seem to evacuate their feelings a bit too easily, and struggle with boundaries and managing difficult feelings. Gillian Rose wrote movingly in her autobiographical fragment that *'to grow in love-ability is to accept the boundaries of oneself and others while remaining vulnerable, woundable, around the bounds'*[42]. Unlike those who can seem cut-off from feelings, some people have strong feelings that overwhelm them, their emotions almost controlling them, the insufficient containment of feelings meaning they spill out.

Janine was the only child of a single mother who had had an abusive upbringing. Janine's mother found parenting hard, had been inconsistent, sometimes absent, sometimes lashing out and sometimes guiltily giving Janine what she wanted. When she was a child, if Janine had a tantrum, her demands would too often be met, whether for sweets, new toys, her mother's attention or anything else.

As she grew older, Janine learnt that she could get what she wanted by making people feel guilty, such as by sulking. She had never learnt to manage frustration, nor to appreciate that others too have needs and feelings. She might fly off the handle when mildly challenged or pout or storm off. She had few friends and people quickly became wary of her. She was easily overwhelmed and flooded by feelings and would desperately get others to try to meet her needs.

Jamie was a 15-year-old from a violent home, with neglectful, drug-using parents. He had been humiliated, physically abused and sometimes ignored while at other times spoiled. In school and in his foster home he was hyper-reactive, quickly flying off the handle, not able to regulate his feelings and getting into conflict too easily.

Janine and Jamie are people who struggled to control their emotions, and instead seemed to be controlled by forces bigger than them. These forces have a powerful effect on the people around them too. A description one psychoanalyst made of such people was of 'being a glass of water without the glass'[43], seemingly raw emotion overflowing with no modulating self that exists to withstand the torrential discharge of emotional states. What used to be called 'high expressed emotion' has generally been seen in psychiatry as indicating deep-seated problems.

Both Janine and Jamie seemed to lack a self in touch with or able to metabolize their feelings, with little capacity or equipment for emotional containment. From one angle, they might seem to be in touch with their emotions and even be 'getting them out'. In fact, they both used dramatic emotional responses to ward off or defend against less tolerable emotional states, such as being vulnerable or hurt. It was easier for both to feel anger than remorse, fury than anxiety, and neither had developed the tools to manage painful feelings like sadness or guilt. Consequently, such feelings were staved off by jumping into well-trodden dramatic feeling states, including rage, self-pity and aggression. If either Janine or Jamie had been lucky enough to receive help in managing and processing painful experiences and tolerating frustration when very young, their stories might well have been very different.

Such people are often described as *thin-skinned*. They might easily feel hurt and upset, unable to brush-off petty slights, often assuming judgement and criticism where none exists. This is very different from people who are more cut off from their feelings and who might be described as thick- rather than thin-skinned, often building a protective armour against emotional experiences they cannot tolerate, such as through ritualised activity or escaping into an intellectual retreat. In either case, if one's psychic skin is too thick or thin, that is often a sign that in early childhood there was a lack of a parental figure who acted as an external regulator of the child's psychic life, providing a protective membrane, lending their own capacity to contain and process emotions and helping the child to develop their own.

Most people in the therapeutic world agree that we want people to be in touch with their feelings. In this section, we have seen that being in touch with feelings does not mean expressing feelings in an uninhibited way, nor being overwhelmed by feelings which take over. It does mean developing a part of the self that can make sense of, bear, process and modulate emotional states, in effect a capacity for emotional containment.

9. THROWING STONES FROM GLASS HOUSES

How the concept of projection helps us understand a way that people can disown emotional experiences.

One should examine oneself for a very long time before thinking of condemning others.
Moliere[44]

As we have seen, some feelings feel too much to bear, and we do our utmost to rid ourselves of them. A young woman, Martha, grew up feeling aggrieved that her younger brother was the favourite of her family. She had developed a finely-honed awareness of any signs of unfairness and also tried desperately to gain the approval of her parents, determined to regain some of her brother's attention. As she grew up, she often assumed the moral high ground and was quick to condemn behaviour in others that she saw as immoral or wrong. She was understandably tuned in to any hint of injustice and had feelings she was never able to manage. Those around her often felt that they were not quite good enough, her female friends complained that they always felt as if 'their slip was showing', and family, friends and colleagues often felt in the wrong.

Martha herself could act in ways that seemed unscrupulous, being pushy at work and treading on people's toes to get what she wanted. Oddly enough, people often felt rather let down by her. Yet, Martha always seemed able to have a reason for her behaviour and could make those around her feel awkward when she was questioned. She seemed to get even more assertive and critical if anyone challenged her. Martha was someone who had never really felt good about herself, and she tried to manage this by getting rid of self-critical feelings that she found to be burdensome. She convinced herself that it was the others who were bad and the problem and, in this process, she seemed to evoke those bad feelings in others that she could not bear in herself.

This process of disowning aspects of ourselves yet seeing those same traits in others is what we mean by *projection*. Some who feel they should not be angry can be quick to accuse others of aggression and deny their own. An adolescent who is insecure about their identity might be fast to denigrate and criticize another teenager for being uncool. In this way, feelings and emotional states that we cannot manage in ourselves can be placed firmly out there, in others, with the unconscious hope that we do not have to face them. This is sometimes purely a mental event, what psychoanalysis calls an *intrapsychic* process. We see cruelty in others that we are quick to condemn, conveniently forgetting our own capacity to be cruel. Such condemnation might remain confined to our thoughts, having no effect on anyone else.

There is another version of getting rid of unwanted emotional states, which we saw with Martha, and this has more of an effect on other people. It involves getting another to feel our unwanted feelings. This is what is often meant by the slightly unwieldy concept of *projective identification*. Patrick is something of a Lothario, a young man who takes pleasure in seducing young women and then abandoning them, leaving many victims in his all-conquering wake. None of his relationships last more than a few weeks, after which he wriggles out of the situation and flees. It is interesting to question why he does this. On meeting him, people seem to feel a need to please him and even a yearning to be liked by him, and women have often felt that they can be the one to save him from himself. Patrick, at one level, believes that he is looking for a lasting relationship and is unhappy at their continual failure. Yet, if we look a little closer, another story emerges.

Patrick came from a difficult background. His mother was a heroin addict and he was taken into care when he was just three years old. He lived with a series of foster families and in children's homes until adolescence when he remained with one foster family but was never adopted. He clearly did not have an ideal start in life, and his basic needs for intimacy and closeness were not met throughout his first few years. As an infant, he had had had glimpses of genuine intimacy with his mother, which was possibly also sexualised, but she was sadly never able to sustain any ongoing parental emotional presence. Consequently, he had experienced a tantalizing promise of a loving if over-intense bond that was then cruelly whisked away.

I suspect that it is no coincidence that these early experiences of being offered a loving closeness which was then whisked away is the same cycle that his sexual conquests undergo. A feeling that is unbearable is somehow 'put into' someone else, albeit not consciously, and the net result is that the young women's emotional states that he could not bear. Such ways of communicating can become habitual and then give rise to what are called *secondary gains*. Patrick's secondary gain was that he learnt to enjoy the power that came with his conquests. Victims of abuse who then abuse others can similarly start by trying to get rid of their feelings into others, but later this can shift into a secondary gain of enjoying power and control.

Thus, getting rid of unbearable feelings is a common way of managing that which otherwise might seem unmanageable. We often see such processes more clearly in young children. Six-year-old Ben had been teased and taunted by a boy in his street. He warded off his upset but then went home and teased and bullied his younger brother who ended up feeling just what Ben had not wanted to feel. Here, Ben was not managing his own feelings and 'got rid' of them into his brother.

14-year-old Jessica had been to her school's open day and a high-achieving classmate had somewhat cattily derided her art. Jessica left feeling uncreative and rather dull, so it was no coincidence that later she cuttingly attacked her parents' conservative taste in décor and style, accusing them of being dull and bourgeois and unimaginative.

Psychoanalysis would see the ability to manage one's own emotional states rather than having to discharge them into others as a sign of maturity. This requires a bearing of emotions and staying with them, a containing of them rather than fleeing of them. Projecting does not help in the long-term, and the feelings we try to deny generally come back to haunt us. However, life becomes much richer for the likes of Ben or Jessica when they can be helped to own, process and bear their upset rather than trying to get rid of them into others.

Bion's classic psychoanalytic idea of containment is rooted in just such an understanding of how to deal with unmanageable powerful feelings, the kind often experienced in infancy. A distressed infant may try to relieve themselves of unbearable states of mind by, for example, kicking, screaming, crying or banging their head. A parent witnessing this will have all manners of feelings stirred up within themselves, often difficult ones, and might find themselves feeling despairing, hopeless, upset or angry. With luck, a parent can do the hard-emotional work of bearing such projected feelings, processing, metabolizing and making sense of them.

This is challenging but vital emotional work which is at the centre of much psychotherapy too. It is this process of containment which helps others bear their emotions. If my feelings are borne and I know that I am understood, then my feelings are not as overwhelming and I have little need to get rid of them by projecting them into others. Many psychotherapists see such a development of a capacious containing capacity as the core of emotional health, enabling the richness that comes with accepting feelings rather than defending against them, an ability to fold emotional states into our psychological repertoire rather than defending against them.

10. THE EMOTIONAL BODY

How psyche, soma and emotions are profoundly linked.

'Common sense says, we lose our fortune, are sorry and weep; we meet a bear, are frightened and run; we are insulted by a rival, are angry and strike. ..... the more rational statement is that we feel sorry because we cry, angry because we strike, afraid because we tremble, and not that we cry, strike, or tremble, because we are sorry, angry, or fearful, as the case may be. Without the bodily states following on the perception, the latter would be purely cognitive in form, pale, colourless, destitute of emotional warmth.'
William James [45]

I wrote earlier that one could consider the body to be the site of emotions and the mind or psyche to be the site of feelings. Nowadays, it is possible for scientists in laboratories to experimentally stimulate people to feel all kinds of things and see corresponding responses in the brain. Emotions have a bodily counterpart, whether in the brain or in other bodily signs such as shallow breathing.

This raises interesting questions about the relationship between mind and body. There is a tendency in some circles to dismiss unexplained physical symptoms as 'all in the mind'. This is not helpful because in such cases people generally have real physical issues, such as pain from fibromyalgia or breathing problems from high levels of stress. Some physical ailments or disorders can be described as psychosomatic which can wrongly imply that the physical symptom is somehow less than real and only in the mind. A danger that psychotherapists have to be beware of is omnipotently thinking that all such symptoms can be explained psychologically.

Seeing the mind and body as separate has been central to Western intellectual traditions going back at least to Descartes who differentiated the mind or soul from the body. This has been an unfortunate legacy, one which has been challenged by recent findings from neurobiology, perhaps by Damasio particularly. Indeed, many psychoanalysts, such as Winnicott[46], have never ascribed to this distinction. I, too, have been suggesting that emotions are bodily states, seen in reactions such as a tensing of muscles or a tightening of the stomach. Having a feeling is a way of knowing and making sense of such physical reactions. Upset, embarrassment, fear or anger all have physical correlates, though the same physical correlate, such as a racing heart, can be interpreted differently depending on our experiences and familial or cultural preconceptions. That racing heart, for example, might be seen as a feeling of anxiety or of excitement, even if in both cases the bodily sensation is the same.

The baby, Rick, who I mentioned earlier and who was so terrified of the sound of the spin-dryer, gave all kinds of signs of his fear. Yet he did not know that what he was feeling was what we call panic. It took his mother to both alleviate his distress and to make sense of what he was experiencing. There was nothing magical about what his mother did, as emotionally challenging as such parenting tasks might be. Part of what she did was to read the Rick's gestures and bodily state and make sense of them. This is one way of saying that bodily states can be read as signs or symptoms of psychological states, but also that this making sense of them transforms them into feelings that can be understood. As a result of such care, Rick will hopefully become someone who will be better than most at reading his own bodily signs and knowing his emotions.

Increasingly, links have been made between psychoanalytic understanding and research into psychosomatic states[47]. Many adults I work with do not recognize their bodily signs of distress for what they are, whether experiencing nausea or feeling sick to their stomach or having a racing heart. There is much wisdom to be found in everyday language which hint at links between bodily and emotional states, such as feeling sick to one's stomach, or someone being a pain in the neck, having a weight on one's shoulder or getting cold feet; these descriptions are part of our everyday discourse for good reason.

We have seen how some people have very little sense of an emotional life and can seem flat, feelingless and detached. They might dissociate from emotions they cannot manage and are far more likely to suffer from psychosomatic disorders. Experiences which cannot be experienced psychologically often seem to impact the body, and psychotherapists often see physiological (psychosomatic) symptoms disappear when the psychological distress that was being avoided is faced and processed. Indeed, research[48] seems to illustrate what psychoanalytic thought has long argued, that psychosomatic symptoms are sometimes, if by no means always, an example of unprocessed emotional states lodged in the body.

In one case, a client, Petra, who had been abused was having constant stomach pains and other minor ailments. These became worse when I, as her therapist, tried to get her to think about that abuse. Her mind would go fuggy and her stomach become irritated, and she often needed to go to the toilet. When she went into such states, I learnt that my job was to help her re-regulate, to feel safe in her body, to find some sense of ease in the room with me. The idea of thinking about her trauma was still too much at this stage and she retreated into powerful bodily reactions. As time went on, Petra began to be able to face some of her painful memories. She could feel rage about what had happened, remember details without shutting off and develop a clear belief that her experiences should not have happened, that she deserved better. Equipped with these new feelings, such as righteous anger, and an ability to face memories and not be so overwhelmed by them, her physical symptoms started to disappear. This, of course, took many months, but it is a sequence we often see in therapy.

We might notice that someone has become

contracted in their muscles and body, going into what are sometimes called *smooth-muscle* states, in which they are unaware of an emotion which has overwhelmed their capacity for containment, something we saw in Petra's IBS and fuzzy mind. Forms of psychoanalytic therapy like ISTDP[49] specialize in helping people bear and experience feelings that are denied and repressed and, in the process, such smooth-muscle states and emotional shut-down give way to emotional aliveness and a renewed capacity to experience feelings such as anger and grief. We all contract and dissociate at times and go into smooth-muscle states, this being an attempt to push away and not feel an emotional state that might otherwise overwhelm us. This, though, has a downstream effect on ailments or symptoms.

Physical symptoms can disappear with the right psychological help. However, they are real, and if left unattended to for too long, they can have very bad long-term consequences on people's health trajectories. Real physical ailments are not epiphenomena of psychic states. Research is clear that stress, trauma and a range of experiences have real bodily outcomes, in the form even of fatal illnesses such as cancer or heart-disease[50]. We need to take physical symptomatology seriously but also find the courage to know that body and mind are linked, and that psychotherapeutic help can alleviate a wide range of physiological symptoms in cases where those symptoms are related to emotions that are defended against and denied.

11. GET HAPPY

The importance of taking positive emotions seriously.

'Fear at my heart, as at a cup
My life-blood seemed to sip.'
Coleridge, The Ancient Mariner[51]

Psychotherapies, including psychoanalysis, have been accused of being better at helping people to manage unhappiness than at becoming happier. Indeed, Freud is said to have suggested that the aim of psychoanalysis was to change human misery into 'ordinary unhappiness' and that the hoped-for result was the not-massively-ambitious one of helping people to manage both love and work. These are real achievements, not to be underestimated, but some of us feel that there is more to a good life. Psychoanalysis has been great in helping us understand how people defend against painful emotional realities but perhaps less successful in thinking about what makes people feel good, enriched and joyful.

Some people sabotage their own attempts at happiness and are fearful of the risk of reaching out for what is really desired in case it goes wrong. Often, this can be because previous hurt, which they are protecting themselves against, stops them being from fully opening up to real possibilities in the present. Martin met Alison at a party and was very attracted to her. They arranged to meet again and he was excited. However, on this second date, he was extremely nervous and was constantly searching for clues to prove that Allison was less keen on him than he was on her. This made Martin tense, which spoilt the evening and effectively made his worries come true. Martin had recently broken up with a long-term partner, a huge blow to his confidence. It had stirred up feelings about his mother's departure from the family home when he was seven years old and of his very critical father. He had become someone who believed that if he got close to anyone they might leave, or disapprove of him, and as a result he rarely dared to hope that things would work out well.

Martin was rather like the doleful and morose Eyeore in Winnie the Pooh. Where others might see a cup half-full, Martin was a 'half-empty man', always looking on the dark side. He had, for good reason, learnt not to be complacent and to expect the worst early on in his life, as in his experience things inevitably did go wrong. But this belief system, his unconscious predictions of disaster, were having a crippling effect on his life, not allowing him to make use of real opportunities for happier times. Whenever he had a hopeful idea, he always managed to come up with something to counter it, a worry, or a fear, and inevitably his hopes got quashed.

Martin lacked confidence, but this was about more than that. He had developed a personality around staying safe and not expecting much. Martin needed help to allow hope and to experience good feelings rather than kill them off. Where Martin saw danger, another person might have seen opportunity. The psychoanalyst Neville Symington described the unconscious part of the self, which he called the *lifegiver*[52], as driving people towards life, hope and taking the risk of grasping for the good things in life. It can take therapeutic help to begin to face life with hope and confidence, to allow a life giver to come alive and do its work. This requires therapy which does not just aim to help people process painful experience, but also helps to manage happy and positive experiences.

It is sometimes easier to see such traits developing in young children. Five-year-old Stephanie was out in the park with her father. She was trying to climb to the top of a very high climbing frame and had started full of confidence. But now, she was showing signs of caution, looking around for help as her confidence ebbed away. She was on the verge of panicking and giving up. Her father noticed and began to talk to her, saying 'yes, well done, you've done really well, it is scary up there, but I think you can do it, yes, there you go, 3 more steps, yes, just 2 more now, nearly there, what a brave girl, yes, you can do it, wow, well done.' It was fascinating to watch how Stephanie responded. Taking courage from her father, she found new resources within her and succeeded where she believed she would fail. Her lifegiver was most definitely activated! Her ensuing smile of pleasure and look of triumph and achievement was delightful.

Children who have sufficiently good experiences will very quickly learn from them and build up an expectation that they can achieve things, that situations can go well and that they can dare to have hopes. Courage and hope are perhaps rather neglected emotions in psychoanalysis, as are other positive emotional states, yet they are crucial for living a good life. The baby or child whose beaming smile is met with a mirroring grin, whose efforts to reach out and play are reciprocated, is likely to begin to trust that they can really have an impact on the world and that their wishes can come true.

On the other hand, the child who is constantly judged, criticized or ignored will not have such confidence or sense of their own abilities or belief that they can make a difference. The neglected child can easily give up trying and retreat into his or her own world. The parent who is constantly criticizing and carping is likely to have an adverse impact on the confidence of a child. Psychotherapists often helpfully describe people defending against emotional pain, but it can also be true that defences are erected against reaching out for good, hopeful or loving experiences. Depression and upset can be clung to and not let go of, often with the belief that 'better the devil you know'. Sticking with what we know and are familiar with, even if it makes us unhappy, is at least safe and often easier than risking change and the possibility of disappointment or of taking a risk. Yet being fearful and risk-averse can have terrible costs, especially as they undermine the ability to reach out for hope and potential joy and pleasure.

Many psychotherapists, particularly those who

work with children, have come to realize that when children or adults are being tough or boastful or over-exuberant, they are not always defending against painful feelings[53]. Sometimes they are, and then they need help to tolerate an unpalatable reality, such as facing their own sense of inadequacy. But sometimes, they also lack good early experiences that many people take for granted, and they need help to feel good, confident, even proud. Sheila was a 16-year-old who had been in the care system for most of her life. When she arrived for therapy, she would spend a lot of time denigrating others in a rather desperate attempt to bolster her flimsy sense of self-worth. However, in time, she slowly made real progress and there was a subtle but definite change in the way she would 'talk herself up'. It was important that the therapist did not confuse this false form of confidence from a more genuine one, and it was vital that her real if precarious achievements were openly validated and acknowledged. As the child psychotherapist, Anne Alvarez, has helped us see[53], every child at times benefits from feeling that they 'are king of the castle', as long as this is an example of authentically trying out the feeling of being special, rather than defensively trying to make someone else feel bad or bolstering up a false good sense of themselves.

We need to be able to experience joy and exuberance as well as difficulty and all that comes in between. An old saying goes that a person should have two pockets into which they can reach. In one should be the words *'for my sake was the world created'* and in the other *'I am dust and ashes'*[54].

Positive feelings have received a bad press within psychoanalysis, and psychoanalysis has received its own bad press as a result. Within some circles this is changing, as an acknowledgement has grown of the need to foster positive emotional states as well as manage difficult ones. Much as we would hope that people, through therapy, would develop more capacity to tolerate and manage the painful things in life. We would also hope that people would develop the psychological tools and abilities to genuinely enjoy life and take the risk of courageously reaching out for what they have too often thought was beyond their grasp.

12. CONCLUSIONS

Midway along the journey of our life
I. found myself within a gloomy wood.
So hard it is its aspects to describe,
This savage, harsh and fearsome wilderness,
That fear rekindles with the memory …
Yet to recall the good that came of it
I shall set forth all else I there beheld.
Dante, Inferno[55]

Feelings, affects and emotions are at the very heart of psychotherapy and indeed of life in general. A psychoanalytic perspective is unique in emphasizing the centrality of unconscious processes, how unconscious mental and affective life has a profound impact on who we are and how we act. Denying feelings, repressing them, dissociating and projecting them onto others are ways in which painful emotions might be defended against. The repressed and unconscious psychological states might be revealed in bodily reactions as well as in dreams, slips of the tongue, free-associations, projections.

People possess different capacities to deal with emotional experience. If we cannot process and bear an emotional experience, then we often turn to less satisfactory ways of managing, and these often have their own costs, such as addictions, self-harm, acting out violently or in psychosomatic symptoms.

The roots of our emotional capacities and learning to regulate one's emotional life nearly always have their origins firmly in early childhood and depend on being thought about, attuned with, emotionally regulated and understood. The capacity for self-care and understanding our own feelings, for reflecting on our emotional lives, will only develop if one's emotions have been thoughtfully reflected upon by important adults in our lives.

Emotional understanding is vastly different from simply knowing about something in a cognitive or intellectual way. Emotional knowledge is visceral, held within procedural memories which are deeply engrained in our bodies, personalities and nervous systems. Expectations of how social interactions are likely to go are laid down early and become unconscious and as natural to us as skills like driving a car or tying a shoelace.

The therapeutic task is partly to notice and make sense of such emotional patterns as they arise in a therapy, indeed often in how they are re-evoked towards and with a therapist. The distrustful person is likely to show profound distrust of their therapist, intimate partner or friends, just as the person who needs to please others will try to win favour with the people in their lives, including their therapist. Change and healing occur when such old patterns are understood, not just in our heads but on an emotional, embodied level. Once understood in this visceral, bodily and also mental way, doors open for new patterns to emerge, as new trains of associations, new networks of neuronal pathways, are set in motion. This is never just an intellectual process. It is a profoundly emotional one, often fraught with discomfort and anxiety as well as, hopefully, excitement, joy and a rekindling of passion and hope. It is a lifegiver moving us towards novel experiences with eager anticipation.

Self-reflection, thinking about and processing emotions, plays a central part in this. The idea of self-reflection presupposes a part of the self that can stay with and process emotions. Some people, sadly, like the thin-skinned characters mentioned earlier, have little sense of their own self. Again, we know from years of research that some parents are more likely to have children who are securely attached, and these are parents who can reflect on their own lives and who can put together a coherent story about their childhood experiences without getting too emotionally triggered and who do not need to deny emotionally-laden experiences. They can do this because they have been fortunate enough to have good enough experiences of being attuned to, generally early on in life but also sometimes later, such as with friends or therapists.

These people have what is sometimes called a capacity for *mentalizing*, or in other words, they can be open to and reflect on emotional experiences, their own and those of others. When such people become parents, they are much more likely to be able to give a similar quality of thoughtful emotional understanding to their own children. This is also the kind of attention that one would hope psychotherapists give to their patients and friends give to each other. Central to psychoanalysis and its related therapies is how they value the importance of fostering just such a capacity for self-reflection, for containment, for making sense of the emotional vagaries that life throws up. Such therapy does not beget someone who fully understands their unconscious, nor someone who has control of their emotional life. However, it might hopefully result in people more able to read signs of unconscious processes, more able to tolerate and experience a genuine depth and breadth in their emotional lives, more able to manage the vicissitudes of intimacy, pain, joy and equally the mundane, and whose lives are far richer as a result.

Thank you for reading Affect and Emotion by Graham Music.

You can sign up for Graham Music's newsletter and other information, including blogs, publications, and forthcoming events, at https://nurturingnatures.co.uk/sign-up/ or visit his website https://nurturingnatures.co.uk/. Graham can be contacted by email gmusic@nurturingnatures.co.uk or on Twitter or LinkedIn.

It makes more of a difference to authors than you might think, so please consider leaving a review on any site you use, such as Amazon, Bookbub or Goodreads.

Below are Graham Music's other books:

Music, G (2022) Respark: Igniting Hope and Joy after Trauma and Depression. London: Mind-Nurturing Books

Nathanson, A., Music, G. and Sternberg, J. (2021) From Trauma to Harming Others: Therapeutic Work with Delinquent, Violent and Sexually Harmful Children and Young People. Routledge.

Music, G. (2019) Nurturing Children: From Trauma to Growth Using Attachment Theory, Psychoanalysis and Neurobiology. Abingdon, Oxon; New York, NY: Routledge.

Music, G. (2016, 2010) Nurturing Natures: Attachment and Children's Emotional, Social and Brain Development. London: Psychology Press.

Music, G. (2014) The Good Life: Wellbeing and the new Science of Altruism, Selfishness and Immorality. London: Routledge.

DEDICATION

To Sue and Rose

ACKNOWLEDGEMENTS

With thanks to Ivan Ward and all at Icon Books for their support on the original edition, to Jason at Polgarus for the excellent formatting to Lindsay for meticulous proof reading and to Xee Designs for the cover. I am also really grateful for the encouragement, candid comments and lively discussions with colleagues and friends, Anne Alvarez, Melissa Benn, Dilys Daws, Robert Glanz, Paul Gordon, Patrick Heaney and Helen Wright.

REFERENCES

1. Rumi. Selected Poems. London: Penguin Classics; 2004.

2. Damasio AR. The Feeling of What Happens: Body, Emotion and the Making of Consciousness. London: Heineman; 1999.

3. van der Kolk BA. The body keeps the score: memory and the evolving psychobiology of posttraumatic stress. Harv Rev Psychiatry. 1994 Feb;1(5):253–65.

4. Adolphs R, Tranel D, Damasio H, Damasio AR. Fear and the human amygdala. J Neurosci. 1995;15(9):5879–91.

5. Bion WR. A theory of thinking. Melanie Klein Today Dev Theory Pract. 1962;1:178–86.

6. Teicher MH, Samson JA, Anderson CM, Ohashi K. The effects of childhood maltreatment on brain structure, function and connectivity. Nat Rev Neurosci. 2016;17(10):652.

7. Gander M, Buchheim A. Attachment classification, psychophysiology and frontal EEG asymmetry across the lifespan: a review. Front Hum Neurosci. 2015; 9:79.

8. Adams HE, Wright Jr LW, Lohr BA. Is homophobia associated with homosexual arousal? J Abnorm Psychol. 1996;105(3):440.

9. Stowe HB. Uncle Tom's Cabin: 1852. Leipzig: Tauchnitz; 1852.

10. Plath S. Ariel: The restored edition. London: Faber & Faber; 2010.

11. Schore AN. Affect regulation and the origin of the self: The neurobiology of emotional development. New Jersey: Lawrence Erlbaum; 1994.

12. Bowlby J. Attachment and loss. Vol. 1, Attachment. London: Hogarth; 1969.

13. Stern DN. The interpersonal world of the infant. New York: Basic Books; 1985.

14. Aron L. A meeting of minds: Mutuality in psychoanalysis. New York: Analytic Press; 2001.

15. Rosen M, Oxenbury H. We're going on a bear hunt. Walker London; 1989.

16. Hobbes T. Leviathon. London: Andrew Ckooke at the Green Dragon in St. Paul's Church-yard, 1651.

17. Reich W. Character analysis. New York: Farrar, Straus and Giroux; 1945.

18. Mencken HL. Minority Report. New York: AlfredA. Knopf; 1956.

19. Emerson RW. The over-soul. London: Women's Printing Society; 1910.

20. Buber M. Tales of the Hasidim. Berlin: Schocken; 1991.

21. Rumi J. The guest house. C Barks J Moyne AJ Arberry R Nicholson Trans P 109 Essent Rumi San Franc Harper. 1995;

22. Brittain V. Testament of youth: an autobiographical study of the years 1900-1925. London: Weidenfeld & Nicolson; 2009.

23. Dickens C. Charles Dickens: The Essential Collection. New York: Race Point Publishing; 2018.

24. Keats J. The complete poetical works and letters of John Keats. Scudder HE, editor. Boston: Riverside Press; 1899.

25. Spitz RA. Hospitalism—An inquiry into the genesis of psychiatric conditions in early childhood. Psychoanal Study Child. 1945; 1:53–74.

26. Perry BD, Pollard RA, Blakley TL, Baker WL, Vigilante D. Childhood trauma, the neurobiology of adaptation, and Use-dependent" development of the brain: How states" become traits". Infant Ment Health J. 1995;16(4):271–91.

27. Smyke AT, Zeanah CH, Gleason MM, Drury SS, Fox NA, Nelson CA, et al. A randomized controlled trial comparing foster care and institutional care for children with signs of reactive attachment disorder. 2014;169(5):508–14.

28. Bick J, Zhu T, Stamoulis C, Fox NA, Zeanah C, Nelson CA. A Randomized Clinical Trial of Foster Care as an Intervention for Early Institutionalization: Long Term Improvements in White Matter Microstructure. JAMA Pediatr. 2015;169(3):211–9.

29. Moulson MC, Westerlund A, Fox NA, Zeanah CH, Nelson CA. The Effects of Early Experience on Face Recognition: An Event-Related Potential Study of Institutionalized Children in Romania. Child Dev. 2009;80(4):1039–56.

30. Dickinson E. The complete poems. London: Faber and Faber; 2016.

31. Frankl VE. Man's search for meaning. London: Simon and Schuster; 1985.

32. De Brito SA, Viding E, Sebastian CL, Kelly PA, Mechelli A, Maris H, et al. Reduced orbitofrontal and temporal grey matter in a community sample of

maltreated children. J Child Psychol Psychiatry. 2013;54(1):105–12.

33. Henry G. Doubly deprived. J Child Psychother. 1974 Oct 1;3(4):15–28.

34. Hodges J, Steele M, Hillman S, Henderson K. Mental representations and defences in severely maltreated children: A story stem battery and rating system for clinical assessment and research applications. Reveal Inn Worlds Young Child. 2003;240–67.

35. Lawrence DH. Lady Chatterley's Lover and A Propos of'Lady Chatterley's Lover'. Vol. 2. Cambridge: Cambridge University Press; 2002.

36. Keenan B. An evil cradling. New York: Random House; 1993.

37. Horrocks R. Male myths and icons: Masculinity in popular culture. London: Palgrave Macmillan; 1995.

38. Hoffman E. Lost in Translation: A Life in a New Language. London: Penguin; 1990.

39. McDougall J. Theaters of the body: A psychoanalytic approach to psychosomatic illness. London: Free Association Books; 1989.

40. Bollas C. The Shadow of the Object: Psychoanalysis of the Unthought Known. London: Free Association Books; 1987.

41. Roth P. Portnoy's Complaint. 1969. N Y Vintage. 1994;

42. Rose G. Love's work. New York. New York Review of Books; 2011.

43. Bromberg PM. Standing in the spaces: Essays on clinical process, trauma, and dissociation. New York: Analytic Press; 1998.

44. Molière JB. Le médecin malgré lui. BoD-Books on Demand; 2019.

45. James W. The principles of psychology. London: Macmillan; 1890.

46. Winnicott DW. Mind and Its Relation to the Psyche-Soma*. Br J Med Psychol. 1954;27(4):201–9.

47. Aron LE, Anderson FSE. Relational perspectives on the body. New York: Analytic Press; 1998.

48. Abbass A. Reaching Through Resistance: Advanced Psychotherapy Techniques. Kansas: Seven Leaves Press; 2015.

49. Davanloo H. Techniques of short-term dynamic psychotherapy. Psychiatr Clin North Am. 1979;2(1):11–22.

50. Felitti VJ, Anda RF. The relationship of adverse childhood experiences to adult medical disease, psychiatric disorders, and sexual behaviour: Implications for healthcare. Impact Early Life Trauma

Health Dis Hidden Epidemic. 2010;77–87.

51. Coleridge ST. The Rime of the Ancient Mariner and other poems. Houghton, Mifflin; 1895.

52. Symington N. Narcissism: A new theory. London: Karnac Books; 1993.

53. Alvarez A. Live company. Oxford: Routledge; 1992.

54. Kopp S. Guru. Palo Alto Calif Sci Behav Books. 1971;

55. Rossetti DG. The Collected Works of Dante Gabriel Rossetti. London: Ellis and Scrutton; 1886.

www.ingramcontent.com/pod-product-compliance
Lightning Source LLC
Chambersburg PA
CBHW050304120526
44590CB00016B/2478